I W

The Sahara is Cold at Night

and other questions about deserts

Jackie Gaff

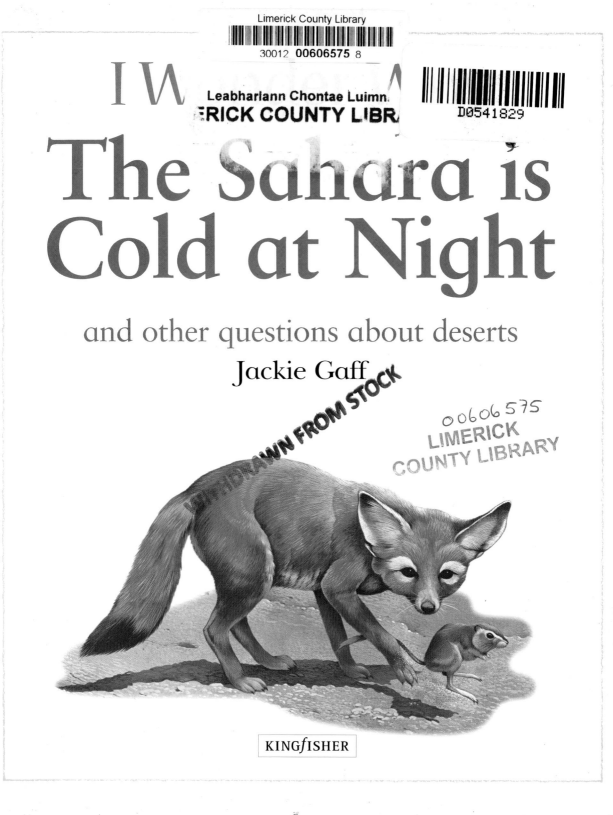

KING*f*ISHER

KINGFISHER
Kingfisher Publications Plc,
New Penderel House,
283–288 High Holborn,
London WC1V 7HZ
www.kingfisherpub.com

First published by Kingfisher Publications Plc 2002
First published in this format 2004
10 9 8 7 6 5 4 3 2 1

1TR/0204/SHE/UNV(RNB)/126.6MA(F)

A CIP catalogue record for this book is available
from the British Library

ISBN 0 7534 0951 8

Series designer: David West Children's Books
Author: Jackie Gaff
Consultant: Keith Lye
Illustrations: James Field (SGA) 5br, 8–9b, 22, 25tr,
    27tr, 30–31; Chris Forsey 10-11, 20, 21tl,
    28–29; Mike Lacey (SGA) 4–5m, 9tr, 24m,
    25b, 26; Mick Loakes 15bl; Steven Sweet 6–7,
    24bl;   David Wright 12–13, 14, 15tr, 15mr,
    16–17, 18-19, 21tr; Peter Wilkes (SGA)
    all cartoons.

Printed in Taiwan

CONTENTS

What is a desert?

Deserts are the driest parts of the world – places where it hardly ever rains. Most have less than 25 cm of rain a year – a tenth of the rain that falls every year in rainforests, the wettest parts of the world.

● Deserts aren't just the world's driest places. They're also the windiest.

Are all deserts hot?

In many of the world's deserts, it is hot enough in the daytime to fry an egg on a rock. Not all deserts are like this, though. Some deserts have baking hot summers and freezing cold winters, while others are chilly all year round.

● Even if you're heading for a hot desert, remember to pack a jumper. Although the daytime temperature can soar to over 40°C, it can drop to below 0°C at night. Brrrrrr!

● When it does rain in a desert, it can bucket down. All of a desert's annual rain may fall in one tremendous storm over two or three days.

● Even a sandy desert may be dotted with big rocks here and there. This huge boulder casts welcome shade during the hottest part of the day – time for people to shelter from the Sun's frizzling heat.

Are all deserts sandy?

No – some are gravelly, while others are rocky or even snowy. Antarctica is a cold snowy desert, for example, where there is no rain and little sun.

● Some deserts are a crazy paving pattern of dried-up salt flats – with a surface that's as hard as concrete.

Where is the world's biggest desert?

The largest desert in the whole world is the Sahara in North Africa. It's larger than Australia, and nearly the size of the entire USA.

- About one fifth of all the land on Earth is desert.

Key to map

■ **The driest deserts, where it hardly ever rains**

■ **Deserts that have enough rain for some plants to grow**

□ **Semi-deserts, with enough rain for shrubby plants to grow**

- At 86 m below sea level, the Death Valley desert is the lowest place in the USA.

FOR SALE

NORTH AMERICA

Great Basin

Mojave

Sonoran

Chihuahuan

ATLANTIC OCEAN

Equator

SOUTH AMERICA

Sechura

Atacama

Patagonian

- South America's Atacama Desert is the world's driest place. Parts of the Atacama had no rain at all between 1570 and 1971 – that's 401 years!

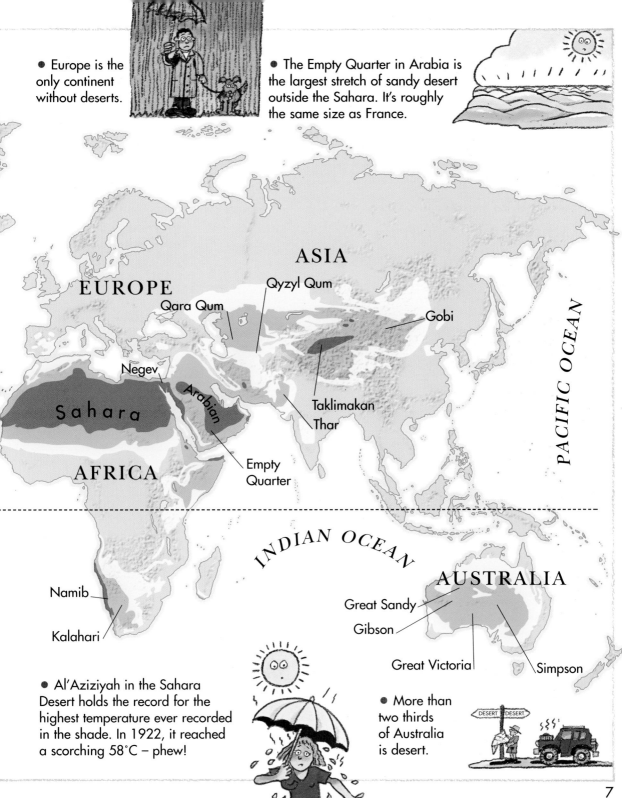

● Europe is the only continent without deserts.

● The Empty Quarter in Arabia is the largest stretch of sandy desert outside the Sahara. It's roughly the same size as France.

ASIA

EUROPE

Qyzyl Qum

Qara Qum

Gobi

Negev

Sahara

Arabian

Taklimakan

Thar

AFRICA

Empty Quarter

PACIFIC OCEAN

INDIAN OCEAN

AUSTRALIA

Namib

Great Sandy

Kalahari

Gibson

Great Victoria

Simpson

● Al'Aziziyah in the Sahara Desert holds the record for the highest temperature ever recorded in the shade. In 1922, it reached a scorching 58°C – phew!

● More than two thirds of Australia is desert.

DESERT DESERT

Why are deserts sandy?

● Strong desert winds sometimes stir up huge clouds of sand. The wind-blown sand is powerful enough to strip the paint from a car.

Sandy deserts are formed mainly by the wind. As it howls across the land, the wind blasts at the rock, wearing it away. Slowly, the rock cracks into stones and pebbles, which over the ages crumble into tiny sand grains.

How high are the tallest sand dunes?

Desert sand dunes come in many shapes and sizes, from camel-high bumps to steep-sided hills. The highest ones measure well over 300 metres – more than twice as high as Egypt's tallest pyramid!

Where can you find mushroom-shaped rocks?

In a desert, of course! The wind carves rocks into all sorts of weird and wonderful shapes as it howls away at them.

● At sunrise and sunset, the rocks and sand of the USA's Painted Desert gleam a rainbow of colours – from blue and violet to golden yellow, brown and red.

● As the sand of a dune shifts and slips, it can give out strange booming or singing noises – spooky!

● Some sand dunes are shaped like a crescent moon...

● ...while others look like a star.

● An S-shaped sand dune is called a 'seif', from the Arabic word for sword.

What is an oasis?

Although little water falls as rain in a desert, there are places where it rises to the surface from deep below the ground. If there's enough water all year round for plants to grow, we call that place an oasis.

● A qanat is a deep underground tunnel carved out by people to bring water into the desert.

When is there water in a wadi?

A wadi is a desert river valley, and most of the time it's as dry as a bone. When there's a rainstorm, however, the wadi fills quickly, and for a while it becomes a roaring, raging torrent of water.

● Every year in the Australian desert town of Alice Springs, people race up the dry bed of the Todd River carrying bottomless boats!

How does sunlight trick desert travellers?

There's nothing a thirsty desert traveller wants to see more than water. But sometimes the shimmering blue pool up ahead isn't water at all – it's just an image of the sky. These tricks of the light are called mirages.

Cool air

Light bending

Warm air

Mirage

● A mirage happens when sunlight is 'bent' as it travels through hot air near the ground. The scientific name for this 'bending' is refraction.

11

How do plants survive in deserts?

All living things need water to survive, so coping with dry desert weather is tough for plants and animals. Plants slurp up water through their roots, and some desert plants have very long roots that dive deep down under the ground.

● The roots of the mesquite bush can tap water as far as 30 metres below the ground.

● When desert plants do get water, they hang on to it. Some use their leaves like a water bank, while cactuses store it in their fat juicy stems.

Why are cactuses spiny?

A cactus' spines are like a barbed-wire fence. They protect the plant and stop most animals from eating it.

• The tallest cactus is the giant saguaro. It can grow to a whopping 12 metres – taller than four camels!

When does the desert burst into flower?

Some desert plants don't bother to grow at all unless it rains. When there is a storm, the seeds sprout, grow and bloom within a matter of weeks, turning the dusty desert into a colourful flowering meadow.

• Instead of spines, some cactuses are camouflaged to hide them from animals. Stone cactuses look just like pebbles.

• The welwitschia of the Namib Desert looks more dead than alive. Don't be fooled, though. It can live for as long as 2,000 years.

How long can a camel last without water?

Camels can go for days without water – weeks if they find enough juicy plants to eat. When a camel gets a drink, it can gulp down 100 litres in ten minutes.

• There are two kinds of camel. Arabian camels have one hump, while the Bactrian camels of Asia have two.

• A camel can go for weeks without food because its hump is like a backpack, where food is stored as fat.

• Many desert lizards store fat in their tails.

Which desert animals never drink?

Jerboas (right) and kangaroo rats don't drink. They get all the water they need from plant seeds and other food.

Can toads live in the desert?

• Nearly all other toads live in wet, watery places because they're amphibians – animals that have to lay their eggs in water.

One kind of toad has a cunning way of surviving the desert drought. For most of the year, the American spadefoot toad keeps its cool in a deep underground burrow. It only comes out to lay its eggs during the rainy season.

• Foggy mornings give the darkling beetle of the Namib Desert all the water it needs. When it tips up its back, water droplets trickle down into its mouth.

• The male sandgrouse is a flying water bottle. When it finds a pool, it uses its fluffy breast feathers like a sponge, to soak up water to carry home to its chicks.

How do desert foxes keep their cool?

The kit fox's big ears work like radiators, giving off heat and cooling its body down. They also help it to listen out for enemies such as hyenas.

● The jack rabbit is another desert animal with big ears to help it keep cool.

Which animal has its own sun parasol?

Unlike most other small desert animals, ground squirrels spend their days out in the Sun. They shelter from the midday heat under their own sun parasols – their tails!

● Many ground squirrels also use their tails for signalling to each other if danger is near.

• The golden mole spends most of its life burrowing through the sand. It can tunnel more than 4 km in one night.

• Many desert animals have light-coloured fur, which helps keep them cool by reflecting sunlight.

Why do desert animals love the dark?

• The elf owl shelters from the hot desert sunlight in a hole in a tall saguaro cactus.

It's a lot cooler out of the Sun than in it, so many small desert animals shelter from the daytime heat in underground burrows. They come out to hunt for food at night, or in the early morning and evening.

How do rattlesnakes kill their prey?

An attacking rattlesnake is lightning fast. It opens its mouth wide, swings its fangs forwards, then bites to inject a deadly poison through them. Small victims die within seconds.

● Rattlesnakes are named for the rattling noise they make by shaking the tip of their tail.

Which desert lizards are poisonous?

Hundreds of different lizards live in deserts, but only two are poisonous – the USA's gila monster and the Mexican beaded lizard. Don't worry, though. These lizards mainly use their poison to protect themselves from enemies, not to attack prey.

Why do scorpions have a sting in their tail?

Scorpions inject poison through their tails, but only if they're really cheesed off. Usually, they just use their claws to catch and kill prey. Scorpions have small eyes and don't see all that well, so they usually track prey using their senses of touch and smell instead.

● The chuckwalla lizard protects itself from enemies by squeezing into a crack in the rock and puffing its body up with air. It's as hard to pull out as a cork from a bottle.

● Scorpions eat insects and spiders mainly, but large scorpions will eat lizards and mice.

19

How do people live in the desert?

Desert survival is all about finding enough water and food to stay alive. Some desert people move from place to place all the time, following good sources of water and food. These travelling people are called nomads.

● The San people of the Kalahari Desert are so expert at tracking down water, they can find small pockets of it under the sand. They suck up the water through a reed straw and store it in an ostrich shell.

What do nomadic people find to eat?

Few desert nomads hunt for wild food these days. Instead, most keep their own herds, so they can drink the animals' milk or make it into cheese.

Who ate ants?

In the past, the nomadic Aboriginal people of the Australian deserts survived entirely by hunting and finding wild food – everything from kangaroos to lizards, insects and plants.

Sweet things were rare, so finding a nest of honeypot ants was an extra-special treat.

● When rains make the desert bloom, honeypot ants feed on sugary nectar from flowers. Some ants store the nectar in their bodies, turning themselves into living honeypots.

● The Tuareg are nomadic herders who live in the Sahara Desert. Their name means the 'people of the veil' – the men's faces are almost completely hidden by their veil-like turbans.

● Nomadic peoples do not move on every day – only when they need fresh supplies of water or food.

Why do desert people build mud houses?

Mud is a fantastic building material. Homes with thick mud walls stay cool inside when the sun is baking hot outdoors, and warm inside if the weather turns chilly. Best of all, mud is dirt cheap – you just have to dig it up.

● Homes can be built from layers of clay mud, or from bricks made by mixing mud with straw or animal hair.

Are there towns in the desert?

There certainly are. Although, in the past, thousands of desert people led a nomadic way of life, very few do today. Most live around oases, or in river valleys such as the Nile, or on the desert fringe.

What is a yurt?

Travellers need portable homes, and yurts are the traditional round tents of the nomadic Mongol people of the Gobi Desert. They're made from wooden poles covered with felt made from sheeps' wool.

● The tents of the nomadic Bedouin people of the Middle East are covered with cloth woven from goats' hair.

Where do people paint with sand?

● In South America's Nazca Desert, more than 1,200 years ago, people scratched huge pictures of birds and other animals into the stony ground.

The Navajo Indians create beautiful paintings with coloured sands for healing rites and other traditional ceremonies. They live in the southeast of the USA's Great Basin Desert.

Why did Australian explorers import camels?

In February 1861, Robert Burke and William Wills became the first settlers to cross Australia from south to north. They wanted camels to carry their supplies because their route took them straight through the deserts in the continent's heart. But because camels aren't Australian animals, the explorers had to import them from Afghanistan.

Darwin

Burke and Wills die at Cooper Creek camp

Melbourne

● Sadly, Burke and Wills both starved to death on the return journey south. Their companion, John King, survived.

Who made it across the Sahara in a microlight?

British explorer Christina Dodwell did in the 1980s, during her mammoth 11,000 km flight across Africa. Her tiny flying machine was called *Pegasus*, after the winged horse of ancient Greek legend.

Which desert explorer carried water in his boots?

Swede Sven Hedin nearly died of thirst when he travelled across Asia's Taklimakan Desert in the 1890s. When he at last stumbled across water, two of his companions were dead and the third had given up walking hours before. Hedin saved the third man's life by carrying water back to him in his boots.

● When Chinese monk Hsuan Tsang set off alone into the Gobi Desert in the 600s, almost the first thing he did was to drop his waterbag. He was saved by his horse, which smelled grass growing around a waterhole and led him to safety.

Where do cars race across the desert?

Briton Andy Green became the world's fastest man on wheels in October 1997, when his jet-propelled car *Thrust SSC* reached a mindboggling 1,227.9 km/h. He set the record on the smooth, flat surface of the USA's Black Rock Desert.

● In January every year, drivers dice with death racing through the Sahara Desert during the Paris to Dakar rally. In 1983, 40 drivers had to be rescued after losing their way during a terrible sandstorm.

● The *Sojourner* rover was tested in US deserts before its launch to Mars, where it landed in 1997.

Why are Space rovers tested in the desert?

Being in a desert is the nearest you can get on Earth to experiencing what it's like on Mars. And that makes a desert the ideal place for putting a Space rover through its paces.

Which is the world's toughest foot race?

You have to be made of tough stuff to enter the Marathon of the Sands. This foot race takes place in the Sahara Desert, with runners covering around 230 km in six days – that's further than five normal marathons!

● Although the temperature can reach 45°C at midday, the Saharan runners have to carry food, clothes and everything else they need – apart from a tent.

● Camels are raced like horses in the Arabian deserts. Their top speed is well over 30 km/h.

Is there treasure in the desert?

Yes – gold, silver and diamonds have all been found in deserts. One of the world's largest diamond mines is in the Kalahari Desert.

● Salt was as precious as gold in ancient times, and there were salt mines deep in the Sahara Desert.

What is black gold?

People often call oil 'black gold', because it's one of our planet's most valuable natural resources. Finding it on their land has made individual people and entire countries very, very wealthy.

● Much of the world's oil is drilled from rocks deep beneath the Arabian deserts.

How can deserts give us clean energy?

Solar power stations are places where the Sun's heat is used to generate electricity. They're much cleaner than a power station that burns oil or coal, and hot deserts are the ideal places to build them.

● Treasure doesn't always glitter. In 1923, American archaeologists were the first to discover fossilized dinosaur eggs in the Gobi Desert. The eggs were later sold for thousands of dollars.

● The world's largest solar power station is in the USA's Mojave Desert.

Did grass ever grow in the Sahara Desert?

Climates change gradually. Thousands of years ago the Sahara was far wetter, with grass to feed animals. We know this because there are fossils and ancient rock paintings which show that cows, antelopes, giraffes and elephants once lived there.

What turns green land into desert?

Overfarming is a major culprit. Plant roots bind soil, stopping the wind blowing it away. When people farm too many animals on the desert fringe, the animals eat all the plants, the soil disappears, and the land becomes desert.

● Deserts also spread if the climate changes, bringing far less rain.

- The rock paintings also show people swimming in ancient Saharan rivers and lakes, as well as water animals such as hippopotamuses and crocodiles.

Can deserts be changed into green fields?

Huge watering projects are one way of turning deserts green again. In parts of North Africa the sand is dotted with round fields, created by gigantic spinning sprinklers.

- In some parts of Arabia, the leftovers from refining oil are sprayed on sand dunes. The grey muddy mixture holds water, allowing plants to grow.

Index